Especially for

_____

From

_____

Date

_____

A Touch of
Comfort

Helen Steiner Rice

BARBOUR
PUBLISHING

Cover design: Greg Jackson, Thinkpen Design

Published by Barbour Publishing, Inc., P.O. Box 719, Uhrichsville, Ohio 44683, www.barbourbooks.com

Our mission is to publish and distribute inspirational products offering exceptional value and biblical encouragement to the masses.

 Member of the
Evangelical Christian
Publishers Association

Printed in China.

Contents

God's Care

The LORD will keep you from all harm—
he will watch over your life; the LORD will
watch over your coming and going both now
and forevermore.

PSALM 121:7–8

God loves you—really, really loves you! And like any loving parent, He has placed caring for you at the top of His list. When you run to Him, you will always find His arms open wide. You can be sure that He will always do what is best for you. You are not alone, dear friend; the great "I Am" is watching over you.

We are all God's children
and He loves us, every one.
He freely and completely forgives
all that we have done,
Asking only if we're ready
to follow where He leads,
Content that in His wisdom
He will answer all our needs.

Somebody cares and always will—
The world forgets,
    but God loves you still.
For God forgives until the end—
He is your faithful, loyal friend.

Our Father in heaven always
knows what is best,
And if you trust in His wisdom,
your life will be blessed.

Oh, God, look down on our cold
hearts and warm them
with Your love,
And grant us Your forgiveness
which we're so unworthy of.

This is how God showed his love among us:
He sent his one and only Son into the world
that we might live through him.

1 John 4:9

He's ever-present and always there
To take you in His tender care
And bind the wounds
  and mend the breaks
When all the world
  around forsakes.

When you're overwhelmed with fears
And all your hopes are
    drenched in tears,
Think not that life has been unfair
And given you too much to bear,
For God has chosen you because,
With all your weaknesses and flaws,
He feels that you are worthy of
The greatness of His wondrous love.

Place yourself in His loving care,

And He will gladly help you bear

Whatever lies ahead of you,

For there is nothing God can't do.

I cannot dwell apart from You,
You would not ask or want me to,
For You have room within Your heart
To make each child of Yours a part
Of You and all Your love and care,
For You are love and Your love should
be everywhere.

There are many things in life that
   we cannot understand,
But we must trust God's judgment
   and be guided by His hand;
And all who have God's blessings
   can rest safely in His care,
For He promises safe passage
   on the wings of faith and prayer!

There's a lot of comfort in the
   thought that sorrow, grief,
   and woe
Are sent into our lives sometimes
   to help our souls to grow. . . .
For through the depths of sorrow
   comes understanding love,
And peace and truth and comfort
   are sent from God above.

Just close your eyes
*   and open your heart*
And feel your worries
*   and cares depart....*
Yield yourself to the
*   Father above*
And let Him hold you
*   secure in His love.*

Put your hope in God,
for I will yet praise him,
my Savior and my God.

Psalm 42:5–6

I come to You frightened and
    burdened with care,
So lonely and lost and so filled
    with despair,
And suddenly, Lord,
    I'm no longer afraid—
My burden is lighter and
    the dark shadows fade.
Oh, God, what a comfort
    to know that You care
And to know when I seek You,
    You'll always be there.

You're worried and troubled
   about everything,
Wondering and fearing what
   tomorrow will bring.
There is only one place
   and only one Friend
Who is never too busy,
   and you can always depend
On Him to be waiting,
   with arms open wide,
To hear all the troubles
   you came to confide.
For the heavenly Father will
   always be there
When you seek Him and find Him
   at the altar of prayer.

At times like these
  man is helpless. . . .
It is only God who can speak
  the words that calm the sea,
Still the wind,
  and ease the pain. . . .
So lean on Him and you will
  never walk alone.

God is no stranger
    in a faraway place—
He's as close as the wind
    that blows 'cross my face.
It's true I can't see the wind
    as it blows,
But I feel it around me,
    and my heart surely knows
That God's mighty hand
    can be felt everywhere,
For there's nothing on earth
    that is not in God's care.

God's Peace

And the peace of God, which transcends all understanding, will guard your hearts and your minds in Christ Jesus.

PHILIPPIANS 4:7

The whole world longs for peace—peace of mind, peace of heart, peace in the world around us. Where can you find it? One place only—in the presence of our Lord Jesus. His peace will surround you, but it will also permeate you, bringing comfort and calm. Even in the midst of life's most powerful storms, you will be unshaken.

After the clouds, the sunshine

After the winter, the spring

After the shower, the rainbow—

For life is a changeable thing,

After the night, the morning

Bidding all darkness cease,

After life's cares and sorrows,

The comfort and sweetness of peace.

God bless you most abundantly
with joys that never cease,
The joy of knowing that He came
to bring the whole world peace.

So kneel in prayer in His presence
and you'll find no need to speak
For softly in quiet communion,
God grants you the peace that
you seek.

God, be my resting place
    and my protection
In hours of trouble, defeat,
    and dejection.
May I never give way to
    self-pity and sorrow,
May I always be sure of
    a better tomorrow.
May I stand undaunted,
    come what may,
Secure in the knowledge
    I have only to pray
And ask my Creator
    and Father above
To keep me serene
    in His grace and His love.

Cast your cares on the Lord

and he will sustain you.

Psalm 55:22

Do not be anxious, said our Lord,
Have peace from day to day—
The lilies neither toil nor spin,
Yet none are clothed as they.
The meadowlark with sweetest song
Fears not for bread or nest
Because he trusts our Father's love,
And God knows what is best.

I know He stilled the tempest
  and calmed the angry sea,
And I humbly ask if in His love
  He'll do the same for me;
And then I just keep quiet
  and think only thoughts of peace,
And if I abide in stillness
  my restless murmurings cease.

When your nervous network
  becomes a tangled mess,
Just close your eyes in silent prayer
  and ask the Lord to bless
Each thought that you are thinking,
  each decision you must make,
As well as every word you speak
  and every step you take—
For only by the grace of God
  can you gain self-control,
And only meditative thoughts
  can restore your peace of soul.

This brings you a million
  good wishes and more
For the things you cannot
  buy in a store—
Like faith to sustain you
  in times of trial,
A joy-filled heart and a happy smile,
Contentment, inner peace, and love—
All priceless gifts from God above!

May peace and understanding
Give you strength and courage, too,
And may the hours and
   the days ahead
Hold a new hope for you;
For the sorrow that is yours today
Will pass away and then
You'll find the sun of happiness
Will shine for you again.

If we but had the eyes to see
    God's face in every cloud,
If we but had the ears to hear
    His voice above the crowd,
We'd find the peace we're seeking,
    the kind no man can give—
The peace that comes from knowing
    He died so we might live!

Take the Savior's loving hand
And do not try to understand—
Just let Him lead you
    where He will,
Through pastures green
    and waters still,
Though the way ahead seems steep,
Be not afraid for He will keep
    tender watch through
    night and day,
And He will hear each prayer
    you pray.

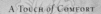
*"Come to me, all you who
are weary and burdened,
and I will give you rest."*

Matthew 11:28

When life becomes a problem
much too great for us to bear,
Instead of trying to escape,
let us withdraw in prayer—
For withdrawal means renewal
if we withdraw to pray
And listen in the quietness to
hear what God will say.

Silently the green leaves grow,
In silence falls the soft, white snow,
Silently the flowers bloom,
In silence sunshine fills a room—
Silently bright stars appear,
In silence velvet night draws near,
And silently God enters in
To free a troubled heart from sin.

God's Provision

Delight yourself in the LORD and he
will give you the desires of your heart.
PSALM 37:4

God is your provider, and He takes that
job seriously. He will not disappoint those
who trust in Him. In fact, He often answers
before you can even ask. His provision may
not come in the way you expect, but it will
always be what you really need. He sees
every situation from beginning to end, and
He provides accordingly. Find comfort in
your Father's unfailing care.

More than hearts can imagine
　　or minds comprehend,
God's bountiful gifts
　　are ours without end.
We ask for a cupful
　　when the vast sea is ours,
We pick a small rosebud
　　from a garden of flowers,
We reach for a sunbeam
　　but the sun still abides,
We draw one short breath
　　but there's air on all sides.

Whatever we ask for
 falls short of God's giving,
For His greatness exceeds
 every facet of living.
Just give Him a chance
 to open up His treasures,
And He'll fill your life
 with unfathomable pleasures.

Always God's ready
*   and eager and willing*
To pour out His mercy,
*   completely fulfilling*
All of man's needs for peace,
*   joy, and rest,*
For God gives His children
*   whatever is best.*

God has a storehouse just
 filled to the brim
With all that man needs,
 if we'll only ask Him.

Trouble is something
  no one can escape—
Everyone has it in some form
  or shape.
But the wise man accepts
  whatever God sends,
Willing to yield like a
  storm-tossed tree bends,
Knowing that God never
  made a mistake,
So whatever He sends
  they are willing to take.
For the grandeur of life
  is born of defeat,
And in overcoming
  we make life complete.

In a myriad of miraculous ways
God shapes our lives
   and changes our days.
Beyond our will or even knowing
God keeps our spirits
   ever growing. . . .
For lights and shadows,
   sun and rain,
Sadness and gladness, joy and pain
Combine to make
   our lives complete
And give us victory through defeat.

*"Seek first his kingdom and
his righteousness, and all these
things will be given to you as well."*

Matthew 6:33

The Lord is our salvation and
our strength in every fight,
Our redeemer and protector,
our eternal guiding light. . . .

He has promised to sustain us,
He's our refuge from all harms,
And He holds us all securely
in His everlasting arms!

I am the Way, so just follow Me,
Though the way be rough
    and you cannot see.
I am the Truth which all men seek,
So heed not false prophets
    nor the words that they speak.
I am the Life and I hold the key
That opens the door to eternity.
And in this dark world,
    I am the Light
To a Promised Land
    where there is no night.

No matter how big our dreams are
God's blessings are infinitely more,
For always God's giving is greater
Than what we are asking for.

While we cannot understand why
   things happen as they do,
The One who hangs the rainbow
   out has His own plans for you.
And may it comfort you to know
   that you are in His care,
And God is always with you,
   for God is everywhere.

"For I know the plans I have for you,"
declares the LORD, "plans to prosper you
and not to harm you, plans to give
you hope and a future."

JEREMIAH 29:11

Sometimes we come to life's crossroads
    and view what we think is the end,
But God has a much wider vision,
    and He knows it's only a bend—
The road will go on and get smoother,
    and after we've stopped for a rest,
The path that lies hidden beyond us
    is often the part that is best. . . .
So rest and relax and grow stronger—
    let go and let God share your load,
And have faith in a brighter tomorrow—
    you've just come to a bend in the road.

Each day there are showers of blessings
    sent from the Father above,
For God is a great, lavish giver,
    and there is no end to His love. . . .
And His grace is more than sufficient,
    His mercy is boundless and deep,
And His infinite blessings are countless—
    and all this we're given to keep.

Death of a
Loved One

He will swallow up death forever.
The Sovereign Lord will wipe away the
tears from all faces; he will remove the
disgrace of his people from all the earth.

Isaiah 25:8

Is your heart heavy, dear friend, and desperate with grief? God instructs us to comfort our hearts with His promise that this life is not the end. Those who are in Christ have been granted eternal life. It's only a matter of time until you are once again in the presence of your loved one. The separation stings, but it has no permanence. Place your hand in God's hand, and lay your head on His mighty shoulder. He understands.

We are so sad when those we love
Are called to live in that home above.
But why should we grieve
   when they say good-bye
And go to dwell in a cloudless sky?
For they have but gone
   to prepare the way
And we'll join them again
   some happy day.

Through the depths of sorrow
comes everlasting love,
And peace and truth and comfort
are sent from God above.

There is no death without a dawning,

No winter without a spring,

And beyond death's dark horizon

Our hearts once more will sing—

There will be no partings

And time is not counted by years.

Where there are no trials or troubles,

No worries, no cares, and no tears.

God has told us that
  nothing can sever
A life He created to live on forever.
So let God's promise
  soften our sorrow
And give us new strength
  for a brighter tomorrow.

All who believe in God's
    mercy and grace
Will meet their loved ones
    face-to-face,
Where time is endless
    and joy unbroken
And only the words of God's love
    are spoken.

Like pilgrims we wander,
   until death takes our hand,
And we start on the journey to
   God's Promised Land—
A place where we'll find
   no suffering or tears,
Where time is not counted in days,
   months, or years—
And in that fair city
   that God has prepared
Are unending joys
   to be happily shared
With all of our loved ones
   who patiently wait
On death's other side to open the gate.

The LORD is my strength and my shield;
my heart trusts in him, and I am helped.
My heart leaps for joy and I will give
thanks to him in song.

PSALM 28:7

Death is only a stepping-stone
To a beautiful life we have
   never known,
A place where God promised man
   he would be
Eternally happy and safe and free.
When death's angel comes to call
God is so great and we're so small. . . .
And there is nothing you need fear
For faith in God makes
   all things clear.

Today your heart is heavy
with sorrow and grief,
But as days turn to months
may you find sweet relief
In knowing your loved one
is not far away,
But is with you in spirit
every hour of the day.

Love like yours can never end
Because it is the perfect blend
Of joys and sorrows,
    smiles and tears,
That just grow stronger
    through the years.
So think of your loved one
    as living above,
No farther away than your
    undying love,
And now he is happy and free
    once more,
And he waits for you
    at eternity's door.

On the wings of death and sorrow
God sends new hope for tomorrow,
And in His mercy and His grace
He gives us strength to bravely face
The lonely days that stretch ahead
And know our loved one is not dead
But only sleeping and out of sight
Until we meet in that land
    that is always bright.

Our dear ones pass on,
   and we see them no more,
But we know they are waiting
   on some other shore.
Death is just a natural thing
   like the closing of a door,
As we start upon a journey
   to a new and distant shore,
And none need make this journey
   undirected or alone,
For God promised us safe passage
   to this vast and great unknown. . . .

Proclaiming to all
doubting men
That in God all
things live again.

Flowers sleeping 'neath the snow,
Awakening when the
    spring winds blow;
Leafless trees so bare before,
Gowned in lacy green once more;
Hard, unyielding, frozen sod
So softly carpeted by God.
These miracles are all around
Within our sight and touch
    and sound,
As true and wonderful today
As when the stone was rolled away.

"For God so loved the world that
he gave his one and only Son,
that whoever believes in him shall
not perish but have eternal life."

John 3:16

If Death should beckon me
  with outstretched hand
And whisper softly of an
  unknown land,
I shall not be afraid to go,
  for though the path I do not know,
I take Death's hand without a fear,
For He who safely brought me here
Will also take me safely back.

Man is but born to die and arise
For beyond this world
in beauty there lies
The purpose of death
which is but to gain
Life everlasting
in God's great domain. . . .
And no one need make
this journey alone
For God has promised
to take care of His own.

Sickness

*"I will restore you to health and heal
your wounds," declares the LORD.*

JEREMIAH 30:17

God created our bodies to run perfectly,
but when sin entered the world they
became frail—subject to sickness, fatigue,
and injury. One day you will receive the
body God intended for you, perfect and
complete. Until then, God says to call on
Him when your body is ailing.

Ask Him to heal you. Then receive His
comfort. He will always be there for you.

Earthly pain is never too much
If He has bestowed
  His merciful touch
And if you look to Him and pray
He will help you through every day.

It makes me sad to think of you
Filled with pain and discomfort, too,
But I know there's nothing I can do
But talk to the Lord and pray for you.

Seed must be sown to
    bring forth the grain,
And nothing is born
    without suffering and pain,
And God never plows
    in the soul of man
Without intention and purpose
    and plan.

For all things pass,
and this will, too,
And with God's help
you'll come smiling through.

I wish I could wipe away every trace
Of pain and suffering from your face,
But He is great and we are small—
We just can't alter His will at all.
And none of us would want to try
For more and more, as days go by,
We know His plan for us is best
And He will give us peace and rest.

Though the way ahead seems steep
Be not afraid, for He will keep
Tender watch through night and day,
And He will hear each prayer
    you pray.
So place yourself in His loving care,
And He will gladly help you bear
Whatever lies ahead of you,
For there is nothing God can't do.

God can remove our uncertain fear

And replace our worry with

   healing cheer....

So close your eyes and open your heart,

And let God come in and freely impart

A brighter outlook and new courage, too,

As His spiritual sunshine smiles on you.

Blessings come in many guises
   that God alone in love devises.
And sickness
   which we dread so much
Can bring a very healing touch.
And through long hours
   of tribulation
God gives us time for meditation,
And no sickness can be counted loss
That teaches us to bear our cross.

Let us then approach the throne of grace with confidence, so that we may receive mercy and find grace to help us in our time of need.

Hebrews 4:16

I wish I knew the right words to say

To take your troubles all away,

But at times like these we realize

That God who is both kind and wise,

Can do what none of us can do,

And that's to heal and comfort you.

I commend you to His care
And may He hear
   your smallest prayer
And grant returning health to you
As only He alone can do.

He is our Shepherd,
     our Father, our Guide,
And you're never alone
     with the Lord at your side.
So may the Great Physician
     attend you
And may His healing
     completely mend you.

In sickness or health,

In suffering and pain,

In storm–laden skies,

In sunshine and rain,

God always is there

To lighten your way

And lead you through darkness

To a much brighter day.

Sickness and sorrow come to us all,
But through it we grow
and learn to stand tall,
The more we endure
with patience and grace,
The stronger we grow
and the more we can face,
And the more we can face,
the greater our love,
And with love in our hearts
we are more conscious of
The pain and the sorrow
in lives everywhere—
So it is through trouble
that we learn to share.

*"If you believe, you will receive
whatever you ask for in prayer."*

Matthew 21:22

Trials

Cast your cares on the LORD and he will sustain you; he will never let the righteous fall.

PSALM 55:22

Trials are a fact of life; they come to each of us. But God is a cool oasis in the midst of the desert. No matter what you are going through, He is there by your side ready to catch you if you should fall. He knows all that you suffer, and He offers you His comforting hand. "Come, walk with Me," He says. "You can face anything when we are walking through it together."

When you're troubled
    and worried and sick at heart
And your plans are upset
    and your world falls apart,
Remember God's ready and
    waiting to share
The burden you find
    too heavy to bear.
So with faith, let go
    and let God lead the way
Into a brighter
    and less troubled day.

When the fires of life
burn deep in your heart
And the winds of destruction
seem to tear you apart,
Remember God loves you
and wants to protect you
So seek that small haven
and be guided by prayer
To that place of protection
within God's loving care.

Let us face the trouble that is
ours this present minute
And count on God to help us
and put His mercy in it.
And forget the past and future
and dwell wholly on today,
For God controls the future,
and He will direct our way.

Whenever I am troubled
and lost in deep despair,
I bundle all my troubles up
and go to God in prayer.

Things achieved too easily
    lose their charm and meaning, too,
It is life's difficulties and the
    trial-times we go through
That make us strong in spirit
    and endow us with the will
To surmount the insurmountable
    and to climb the highest hill.

Seed must be sown to
    bring forth the grain,
And nothing is born
    without suffering and pain,
And God never plows
    in the soul of man
Without intention
    and purpose and plan.

Do not be anxious about anything,
but in everything, by prayer and petition,
with thanksgiving, present your requests to God.

Philippians 4:6

When trouble comes,
　　as it does to us all,
God is so great
　　and we are so small—
But there is nothing that
　　we need know
If we have faith that wherever we go
God will be waiting to help us bear
Our pain and sorrow,
　　our suffering and care—
For no pain or suffering
　　is ever too much
To yield itself to God's
　　merciful touch.

God is the master builder,
His plans are perfect and true,
And when He sends you sorrow,
It's part of His plan for you. . . .
For all things work together
To complete the master plan,
And God up in His heaven
Can see what's best for man.

While I am sure that You love me still
And I know in my heart that
 You always will,
Somehow I feel that
 I cannot reach You,
And though I get down on my knees
 and beseech You,
I cannot bring You closer to me,
And I feel adrift on life's raging sea. . . .
But though I cannot feel Your hand
To lead me on to the Promised Land,
I still believe with all my being
Your hand is there beyond my seeing.

He has promised to sustain us,

He's our refuge from all harms,

And underneath this refuge,

Are the everlasting arms.

Cast your burden on Him,

Seek His counsel when distressed,

And go to Him for comfort

When you're lonely

　　and oppressed—

For God is our encouragement

In troubles and in trials,

And in suffering and in sorrow

He will turn our tears to smiles.

Growing trees are strengthened
    when they withstand the storm,
And the sharp cut of a chisel
    gives the marble grace and form.
God never hurts us needlessly
    and He never wastes our pain,
For every loss He sends to us is
    followed by rich gain.
So whenever we are troubled
    and when everything goes wrong,
It is just God working in us
    to make our spirits strong.

There is always hope of tomorrow
　to brighten the clouds of today. . . .
There is always a corner for turning,
　no matter how weary the way. . . .
So just look ahead to tomorrow and
　trust that you'll find waiting there
The sunlight that seemed to be
　hidden by yesterday's cloud
　of despair.

But the Lord is faithful, and he will strengthen and protect you.

2 THESSALONIANS 3:3

Soul
Restoration

*"Come to me, all you who are weary
and burdened, and I will give you rest."*
MATTHEW 11:28

We all feel weary at times, ready to give
up. If that's how you feel, God wants you
to know that your own strength may be
small, but His is great. He is waiting, eager
to infuse you with new energy, restore your
vision, and help you carry your burdens.
You are not alone, dear friend. Place all your
burdens on Him and receive rest for your
soul.

Often we pause and wonder
When we kneel down to pray—
Can God really hear
The prayers that we say?
But if we keep praying
And talking to Him,
He'll brighten the soul
That was clouded and dim,
For though we feel helpless
And alone when we start,
Our prayer is the key
That opens the heart.

It's not money or gifts
    or material things,
But understanding
    and the joy it brings,
That can change this old world
    in wonderful ways
And put goodness and mercy
    back in our days.

Keep on believing,
* whatever betide you,*
Knowing that God will
* be with you to guide you. . . .*
And all that He promised
* will be yours to receive*
If you trust Him completely
* and always believe.*

Look ahead to tomorrow and trust
that you'll find waiting there
The sunlight that seemed to be
hidden by yesterday's clouds
of despair.

*The flower of love and devotion has
guided me all through my life;
Softening my grief and my trouble,
sharing my toil and strife.*

While life's a mystery we
    can't understand,
The great Giver of life
    is holding our hand,
And safe in His care
    there is no need for seeing,
For in Him we live and move
    and have our being.

The Lord is my light and my salvation—
whom shall I fear? The Lord is the stronghold
of my life—of whom shall I be afraid?

Psalm 27:1

God has given us the answers,
　　which too often go unheeded,
But if we search His promises,
　　we'll find everything that's needed
To lift our faltering spirits
　　and renew our courage, too,
For there's absolutely nothing
　　too much for God to do.

Thank You, God, for the
    beauty around me everywhere
The gentle rain and glistening dew,
    the sunshine and the air,
The joyous gift of feeling
    the soul's soft, whispering voice,
That speaks to me from deep within,
    and makes my heart rejoice.

The Lord is our salvation and
our strength in every fight,
Our redeemer and protector,
our eternal guiding light.

Each time you smile you'll find it's true
Somebody, somewhere
   will smile back at you,
And nothing on earth
   can make life more worthwhile
Than the sunshine and warmth
   of a beautiful smile.

There is nothing that we need know
If we have faith that wherever we go
God will be waiting to help us bear
Our pain and sorrow, our suffering and care.

The rainbow is God's promise
Of hope for you and me,
And though the clouds hang heavy
And the sun we cannot see,
We know above the dark clouds
That fill the stormy sky,
Hope's rainbow will come
    shining through
When the clouds have drifted by.

His goodness is unfailing,
His kindness knows no end,
For the Lord is a good Shepherd
on whom you can depend.
He will guard and guide and keep
you in His loving, watchful care,
And when traveling in dark valleys,
your Shepherd will be there.

To you, O Lord, I lift up my soul.

Psalm 25:1

Deliverance

The LORD is good, a refuge in times of trouble.
He cares for those who trust in him.

NAHUM 1:7

Don't be frightened, dear friend. The way before you may seem rocky, mysterious, and filled with danger; but you are in the presence of someone much greater than any dark shadow that may cross your path. Even the fiercest enemy is nothing in His eyes. You are safe with Him. Replace your fear with the comfort of His loving smile. Let Him show you what His love can do.

When life seems empty
    and there's no place to go,
When your heart is troubled
    and your spirits are low,
The burden that seems too heavy to bear
    God lifts away on the wings of prayer.

Sometimes the road of life seems long
as we travel through the years
And with a heart that's broken
and eyes brimful of tears,
We falter in our weariness
and sing beside the way,
But God leans down and whispers,
"Child, there'll be another day."

Wish not for the easy way
to win your heart's desire,
For the joy's in overcoming and
withstanding flood and fire—
For to triumph over trouble and
grow stronger with defeat
Is to win the kind of victory that
will make your life complete.

The road will grow much smoother
And much easier to face,
So do not be disheartened—
This is just a resting place.

Another hill and sometimes a mountain
But just when you reach the peak—
Your weariness is lifted
And you find the peace you seek.

He will not let me go alone
Into the valley that's unknown.
Kings and kingdoms
   all pass away—
Nothing on earth endures.
But the love of God
   who sent His Son
Is forever and ever yours.

Teach us that it takes the showers to
   make the flowers grow,
And only in the storms of life
   when the winds of trouble blow
Can man, too, reach maturity
   and grow in faith and grace,
And gain the strength and courage
   to enable him to face
Sunny days as well as rain,
   high peaks as well as low,
Knowing that the April showers
   will make the May flowers grow.

And then at last may we accept
the sunshine and the showers,
Confident it takes them both
to make salvation ours.

This is how God showed his love among us:
He sent his one and only Son into the
world that we might live through him.

1 JOHN 4:9

There are times when life overwhelms us
And our trials seem too many to bear—
It is then we should stop to remember
God is standing by, ready to share
The uncertain hours that confront us
And fill us with fear and despair.

For God in His goodness has promised
That the cross that He gives us to wear
Will never exceed our endurance
Or be more than our strength can bear.

Secure in a blessed assurance
We can smile as we face tomorrow,
For God holds the key to the future,
And no sorrow or care
  we need borrow.

When everything is pleasant and bright
And the things we do turn out just right,
We feel without question that God is real,
For when we are happy, how good we feel,
But when the tides turn and gone is the song
And misfortune comes
    and our plans go wrong,
It is when our senses are reeling
We realize clearly it's faith and not feeling,
For it takes great faith to patiently wait,
Believing God comes not too soon or too late.

What more can we ask of the Savior
Than to know we are never alone—
That His mercy and love are unfailing
And He makes all our problems
  His own.

My blessings are so many,

My troubles are so few,

How can I feel discouraged

When I know that I have You?

And I have the sweet assurance

That I'll never stand alone

If I but keep remembering

I am Yours and Yours alone.

Oh, Father, grant once more to men
A simple childlike faith again,
Forgetting color, race, and creed
And seeing only the
 heart's deep need. . . .
For faith alone can save man's soul
And lead him to a higher goal,
For there's but one unfailing course—
We win by faith and not by force.

"Surely I am with you always,
to the very end of the age."

Matthew 28:20

Grace

It is by grace you have been saved, through faith—
and this not from yourselves, it is the gift of God.

EPHESIANS 2:8

God's unmerited favor—that's what grace is. He loves you, cares for you, comforts and provides for you. . .even though you don't deserve it. Don't waste a moment thinking that you aren't good enough to walk with God. He has made you good enough by allowing His own Holy Son to give His life in exchange for yours. Linger long in God's grace. It is His greatest gift.

Our Father made the heavens,

The mountains and the hills,

The rivers and the oceans,

And the golden daffodils.

How wonderful to contemplate

And know that it is true

That He who planned the universe

Gave us our Savior, too.

Life is change, but never loss
For Christ purchased our salvation
When He died upon the cross.

The more we endure
　　with patience and grace,
The stronger we grow
　　and the more we can face,
And the more we can face,
　　the greater our love,
And with love in our hearts
　　we are more conscious of
The pain and the sorrow
　　in lives everywhere—
So it is through trouble
　　that we learn to share.

His grace is all-sufficient
for both the young and old,
For the lonely and the timid,
for the brash and the bold.

If we place our lives in God's hands

And surrender completely

   to His will and demands,

The darkness lifts and the

   sun shines through,

And by His touch we are born anew.

No one has ever sought the Father
   and found He was not there,
And no burden is too heavy
   to be lightened by a prayer,
No problem is too intricate
   and no sorrow that we face
Is too deep and devastating
   to be softened by His grace.

*"My grace is sufficient for you,
for my power is made perfect in weakness."*

2 Corinthians 12:9

God asks for no credentials,
   He accepts us with our flaws,
He is kind and understanding,
   and He welcomes us because
We are His erring children
   and He loves us every one,
And He freely and completely
   forgives all that we have done.

We all have many things
     to be deeply thankful for,
But God's everlasting promise
     of life forevermore
Is a reason for thanksgiving
     every hour of the day,
As we walk toward eternal life
     along the King's highway.

Where can we find the Holy One?
Where can we see His only Son?
The Wise Men asked,
   and we're asking still,
Where can we find
   this Man of goodwill?
Is He far away in some distant place,
Ruling unseen from
   His throne of grace?
Is there nothing on earth that man can
   see to give him proof of eternity?

Every day somewhere, someplace,

We see the likeness of His face.

For who can watch a new day's birth

Or touch the warm, life-giving earth,

Or feel the softness of the breeze

Or look at skies through lacy trees

And say they've never seen His face

Or looked upon His throne of grace?

Realizing my helplessness,
I'm asking God if He will bless
The thoughts you think and all you do
So these dark hours
    you're passing through
Will lose their grave anxiety,
And only deep tranquility
Will fill your mind and help impart
New strength and courage
    to your heart.

Tender little memories
  of little things we've done
Make the very darkest day
  a bright and happy one.
Tender little memories
  of some word or deed
Give us strength and courage
  when we are in need.

Each day at dawning
   we have but to pray
That all the mistakes
   that we made yesterday
Will be blotted out
   and forgiven by grace,
For God in His mercy
   will completely efface
All that is past,
   and He'll grant a new start
To all who are truly repentant
   at heart.

You believe in him and are filled with
an inexpressible and glorious joy.

1 Peter 1:8

God's Promises

Know therefore that the L<small>ORD</small> your God is God;
he is the faithful God, keeping his covenant of
love to a thousand generations of those who
love him and keep his commands.

D<small>EUTERONOMY</small> 7:9

A promise is of no value unless it is kept.
God keeps His promises—no matter how
great or small. He has instructed us to put
His promises to the test and in so doing
confirm His goodness and His faithfulness.
He will never fail you, dear friend. What
He says He will do, He does. You can
anchor your life on that.

When life seems empty
and there's no place to go,
When your heart is troubled
and your spirits are low,
When friends seem few
and nobody cares—
There is always God
to hear your prayers.

The waking earth in springtime
reminds us it is true
That nothing really ever dies
that is not born anew. . . .
So trust God's all-wise wisdom
and doubt the Father never,
For in His heavenly kingdom
there is nothing lost forever.

The love of God surrounds us
Like the air we breathe
   around us—
As near as a heartbeat,
As close as a prayer,
And whenever we need Him,
He'll always be there!

My blessings are so many,
   my troubles are so few—
How can I be discouraged when
   I know that I have You?
And I have the sweet assurance
   that there's nothing I need fear
If I but keep remembering
   I am Yours and You are near.

We've God's Easter promise,
  so let us seek a goal
That opens up new vistas
  for man's eternal soul. . . .
For our strength and our security
  lie not in earthly things
But in Christ the Lord, who died
  for us and rose as King of kings.

There are many things in life
   that we cannot understand,
But we must trust God's judgment
   and be guided by His hand;
And all who have God's blessing
   can rest safely in His care,
For He promises safe passage
   on the wings of faith and prayer.

God's love endures forever—
  what a wonderful thing to know
When the tides of life run against you
  and your spirit is downcast and low.
God's kindness is ever around you,
  always ready to freely impart
Strength to your faltering spirit,
  cheer to your lonely heart.
God's presence is always beside you,
  as near as the reach of your hand.
You have but to tell Him your troubles—
  there is nothing He won't understand.

God's presence is ever beside you,
    as near as the reach of your hand.
You have but to tell Him your
    troubles—there's nothing He
    won't understand.
And knowing God's love is unfailing,
    and His mercy unending and great,
You have but to trust in His
    promise—God comes not
    too soon or too late.

*Now faith is being sure of what we
hope for and certain of what we do not see.*

HEBREWS 11:1

Death is not sad…
    it's a time for elation,
A joyous transition…
    the soul's emigration
Into a place where
    the soul's safe and free
To live with God through eternity!

When God makes a promise,

It remains forever true,

For everything God promises

He unalterably will do.

When you're disillusioned
And every hope is blighted
Recall the promises of God
And your faith will be relighted,
Knowing there's one lasting promise
On which man can depend,
And that's the promise of salvation
And a life that has no end.

Secure in that blessed assurance,
      we can smile as we face tomorrow,
For God holds the key to the future,
      and no sorrow or care we need borrow.

We know that our Father
will richly provide
All that He promised
to those who believe,
And His kingdom is waiting
for us to receive.

America's beloved inspirational poet laureate, **Helen Steiner Rice**, has encouraged millions of people through her beautiful and uplifting verse. Born in Lorain, Ohio, in 1900, Helen was the daughter of a railroad man and an accomplished seamstress and began writing poetry at a young age.

In 1918, Helen began working for a public utilities company and eventually became one of the first female advertising managers and public speakers in the country. In January 1929, she married a wealthy banker named Franklin Rice, who later sank into depression during the Great Depression and eventually committed suicide. Helen later said that her suffering made her sensitive to the pain of others. Her sadness helped her to write some of her most uplifting verses.

Her work for a Cincinnati, Ohio, greeting card company eventually led to her nationwide popularity as a poet when her Christmas card poem "The Priceless Gift of Christmas" was first read on *The Lawrence Welk Show*. Soon Helen had produced several books of her poetry that were a source of inspiration to millions of readers.

Helen died in 1981, leaving a foundation in her name to offer assistance to the needy and the elderly. Now more than twenty-five years after her death, Helen's words still speak powerfully to the hearts of readers about love and comfort, faith and hope, peace and joy.

*My God will meet all your needs according
to his glorious riches in Christ Jesus.*

PHILIPPIANS 4:19